Susanna Tee

Cupcakes

p

This is a Parragon Publishing Book
First published in 2006

Parragon Publishing
Queen Street House
4 Queen Street
Bath BA1 1HE, UK

ISBN: 1-40547-138-7

Printed in China

Created and produced by the Bridgewater Book Company Ltd
Photographer: Laurie Evans
Home economist: Fergal Connolly

Notes for the Reader

This book uses imperial, metric, or US cup measurements. Follow the same units of
measurement throughout; do not mix imperial and metric. All spoon measurements are level:
teaspoons are assumed to be 5 ml, and tablespoons are assumed to be 15 ml. Unless otherwise
stated, milk is assumed to be whole, eggs and individual vegetables such as potatoes are medium,
and pepper is freshly ground black pepper. Recipes using raw or very lightly cooked eggs
should be avoided by infants, the elderly, pregnant women, convalescents,
and anyone suffering from an illness.

contents

introduction

Who can resist a cupcake, and what is it that makes them so appealing? Why are they loved by children and adults alike? Perhaps it is their size that makes them so tempting—after all, you can have an individual, diminutive cake all to yourself!

There are two main types of cupcake. The simpler sort is made with a plain cake batter and then topped with a frosting. If you would like something a little more elaborate, then you can try making the cake batter with more ingredients added, from chopped nuts to fresh fruit and pieces of chocolate.

There are several theories on the origin of cupcakes, and they probably all have some truth in them. Some people believe that, as these little cakes were originally baked in cups, which is evident in some old cookbooks, this is how they came to be called cupcakes. Other people believe that the name may have come from the amount of the basic ingredients used to make a cake, with the addition of eggs and any flavorings. In Britain,

for example, where the American cup-based measuring convention for ingredients is not used otherwise, old recipes called for a cupful of sugar, a cupful of butter, and a cupful of flour. Nowadays, in both America and Britain, the term "cupcake" is used for a small cake baked in a fluted paper baking case, a cup, or a cup-shaped mold.

Fluted paper baking cases retain the cakes, and help to keep them moist and fresh for longer. The usual sizes for cases are mini, measuring $1\frac{1}{4}$ inches/3 cm; standard, measuring $1\frac{3}{4}$ inches/4.5 cm; and large (muffin), measuring $2\frac{1}{4}$ inches/5.5 cm. They are also available in various colors, the most usual being white or brown, but they are also available in silver, gold, and printed with a decoration. There are even reusable baking cases available, which are made of silicone and are brightly colored. Cupcakes can also be made in flexible ovenware cupcake molds, but these are used without the paper cases and obviously the resulting cupcakes do not look quite the same.

Also look out for different decorations. There are a wide variety of these too, from small silver balls and various chocolates, to candied flowers and elaborate chocolate flowers.

Cupcakes are quick and easy to make and some of the recipes in this book are made by the all-in-one method, where all the ingredients are put in one bowl and beaten together for even quicker results. Many of the recipes suggest using soft margarine but, since there is such a bewildering array of margarines on the market, make sure you choose a soft margarine that is labeled "suitable for baking." These are ideal for whipping up a batch of cupcakes in no time at all. However, for flavor and a natural product, you cannot do better than use butter. If it is rock hard when you want to use it, pop it in the microwave on a high setting for 10 seconds to soften slightly.

If you need a basic recipe to create your own cupcakes, a cake batter made with 8 tablespoons of butter, ½ cup sugar, generous ¾ cup flour, and 2 eggs makes about 12 standard-sized cupcakes. To make a basic chocolate cupcake batter, replace 1 tablespoon of the flour with 1 tablespoon of unsweetened cocoa. Fill the paper cases about two-thirds full and bake in an oven preheated to 350°F/180°C for about 20 minutes. A buttercream frosting made with 6 tablespoons of butter and 1½ cups confectioners' sugar, or glacé frosting made with 1½ cups confectioners' sugar and 2–3 teaspoons of water, is sufficient to top them.

In this book, you are spoilt for choice. There are Family Favorites, such as Sticky Gingerbread Cupcakes; Fruit Cupcakes, all bursting with fruit, such as moist Apple Streusel Cupcakes; and Chocolate Sensations, a chapter of chocolate cupcakes all to themselves! Finally there are Festive Creations for all occasions, from Christmas Cupcakes to The Cupcake Wedding Cake. These are irresistible cakes worthy of any occasion, whether a supper party, a classroom birthday, a cake sale, a Halloween party, or even a wedding. Why not get baking right away?

family favorites

family favorites

Although these are perhaps the simplest of cupcakes, they have been popular since the eighteenth century. In those days they were baked in individual fluted pans and not in paper cases as they are today.

queen cakes

Makes 18 cupcakes

8 tbsp butter, softened, or soft margarine

generous 1/2 cup superfine sugar

2 large eggs, lightly beaten

4 tsp lemon juice

scant 1 1/4 cups self-rising white flour

3/4 cup currants

2–4 tbsp milk, if necessary

★ Preheat the oven to 375°F/190°C. Put 18 paper baking cases in a muffin pan, or 18 double-layer paper cases on a baking sheet.

★ Put the butter and sugar in a bowl and beat together until light and fluffy. Gradually beat in the eggs, then beat in the lemon juice with 1 tablespoon of the flour. Using a metal spoon, fold in the remaining flour and the currants, adding a little milk if necessary to give a soft dropping consistency. Spoon the batter into the paper cases.

★ Bake the cupcakes in the preheated oven for 15–20 minutes, or until well risen and golden brown. Transfer to a wire rack and let cool.

These honey-soaked cupcakes are inspired by the Greek spiced honey cakes known as "Melomakárona." They are for all those with a sweet tooth and, of course, lovers of honey!

drizzled honey cupcakes

Makes 12 cupcakes

scant 5/8 cup self-rising
    white flour

1/4 tsp ground cinnamon

pinch of ground cloves

pinch of grated nutmeg

6 tbsp butter, softened

generous 3/8 cup superfine sugar

1 tbsp honey

finely grated rind of 1 orange

2 eggs, lightly beaten

3/4 cup walnut pieces, minced

Topping

1/8 cup walnut pieces, minced

1/4 tsp ground cinnamon

2 tbsp honey

juice of 1 orange

★ Preheat the oven to 375°F/190°C. Put 12 paper baking cases in a muffin pan, or put 12 double-layer paper cases on a baking sheet.

★ Sift the flour, cinnamon, cloves, and nutmeg together into a bowl. Put the butter and sugar in a separate bowl and beat together until light and fluffy. Beat in the honey and orange rind, then gradually add the eggs, beating well after each addition. Using a metal spoon, fold in the flour mixture. Stir in the walnuts, then spoon the batter into the paper cases.

★ Bake the cupcakes in the preheated oven for 20 minutes, or until well risen and golden brown. Transfer to a wire rack and let cool.

★ To make the topping, mix together the walnuts and cinnamon. Put the honey and orange juice in a pan and heat gently, stirring, until combined.

★ When the cupcakes have almost cooled, prick the tops all over with a fork or skewer and then drizzle with the warm honey mixture. Sprinkle the walnut mixture over the top of each cupcake and serve warm or cold.

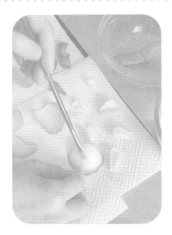

Rose oil extract might seem like an unusual ingredient, but it gives a subtle floral flavor to these little cakes.

rose petal cupcakes

Makes 12 cupcakes

8 tbsp butter, softened

generous ¹/₂ cup superfine sugar

2 eggs, lightly beaten

1 tbsp milk

few drops of extract of rose oil

¹/₄ tsp vanilla extract

scant 1¹/₄ cups self-rising white flour

Frosting

6 tbsp butter, softened

1¹/₂ cups confectioners' sugar

pink or purple food coloring (optional)

silver dragées (cake decoration balls), to decorate

Candied rose petals

12–24 rose petals

lightly beaten egg white, for brushing

superfine sugar, for sprinkling

★ To make the candied rose petals, gently rinse the petals and dry well with paper towels. Using a pastry brush, paint both sides of a rose petal with egg white, then coat well with superfine sugar. Place on a tray and repeat with the remaining petals. Cover the tray with foil and let dry overnight.

★ Preheat the oven to 400°F/200°C. Put 12 paper baking cases in a muffin pan, or put 12 double-layer paper cases on a baking sheet.

★ Put the butter and sugar in a bowl and beat together until light and fluffy. Gradually add the eggs, beating well after each addition. Stir in the milk, rose oil extract, and vanilla extract then, using a metal spoon, fold in the flour. Spoon the batter into the paper cases.

★ Bake the cupcakes in the preheated oven for 12–15 minutes until well risen and golden brown. Transfer to a wire rack and let cool.

★ To make the frosting, put the butter in a large bowl and beat until fluffy. Sift in the confectioners' sugar and mix well together. If wished, add a few drops of pink or purple food coloring to complement the rose petals.

★ When the cupcakes are cold, spread the frosting on top of each cake. Top with 1–2 candied rose petals and sprinkle with silver dragées to decorate.

Unlike many cupcakes, these family favorites will keep for several days in an airtight tin because they are rich, sticky, and moist—if you can resist eating them, that is!

sticky gingerbread cupcakes

Makes 16 cupcakes

generous ³/₄ cup all-purpose flour

2 tsp ground ginger

³/₄ tsp ground cinnamon

I piece of preserved ginger, minced

³/₄ tsp baking soda

4 tbsp milk

6 tbsp butter, softened, or soft margarine

generous ¹/₃ cup firmly packed brown sugar

2 tbsp molasses

2 eggs, lightly beaten

pieces of preserved ginger, to decorate

Frosting

6 tbsp butter, softened

I¹/₂ cups confectioners' sugar

2 tbsp ginger syrup from the preserved ginger jar

★ Preheat the oven to 325°F/160°C. Put 16 paper baking cases in a muffin pan, or place 16 double-layer paper cases on a baking sheet.

★ Sift the flour, ground ginger, and cinnamon together into a bowl. Add the chopped ginger and toss in the flour mixture until well coated. In a separate bowl, dissolve the baking soda in the milk.

★ Put the butter and sugar in a bowl and beat together until fluffy. Beat in the molasses, then gradually add the eggs, beating well after each addition. Beat in the flour mixture, then gradually beat in the milk. Spoon the batter into the paper cases.

★ Bake the cupcakes in the preheated oven for 20 minutes, or until well risen and golden brown. Transfer to a wire rack and let cool.

★ To make the frosting, put the butter in a bowl and beat until fluffy. Sift in the confectioners' sugar, add the ginger syrup, and beat together until smooth and creamy. Slice the preserved ginger into thin slivers or chop finely.

★ When the cupcakes are cold, spread the frosting on top of each cupcake, then decorate with pieces of ginger.

These little cakes are always a favorite with children, but who can resist them when baked in large muffin cases, topped with a swirl of creamy frosting?

frosted peanut butter cupcakes

Makes 16 cupcakes

4 tbsp butter, softened, or soft margarine

generous 1⅛ cups firmly packed brown sugar

generous ⅓ cup crunchy peanut butter

2 eggs, lightly beaten

1 tsp vanilla extract

scant 1⅝ cups all-purpose flour

2 tsp baking powder

generous ⅓ cup milk

Frosting

scant 1 cup full-fat soft cream cheese

2 tbsp butter, softened

2 cups confectioners' sugar

★ Preheat the oven to 350°F/180°C. Put 16 muffin paper cases in a muffin pan.

★ Put the butter, sugar, and peanut butter in a bowl and beat together for 1–2 minutes, or until well mixed. Gradually add the eggs, beating well after each addition, then add the vanilla extract. Sift in the flour and baking powder and then, using a metal spoon, fold them into the mixture, alternating with the milk. Spoon the batter into the paper cases.

★ Bake the cupcakes in the preheated oven for 25 minutes, or until well risen and golden brown. Transfer to a wire rack and let cool.

★ To make the frosting, put the cream cheese and butter in a large bowl and, using an electric hand whisk, beat together until smooth. Sift the confectioners' sugar into the mixture, then beat together until well mixed.

★ When the cupcakes are cold, spread the frosting on top of each cupcake, swirling it with a round-bladed knife. Store the cupcakes in the refrigerator until ready to serve.

Almonds are often the first choice of nut when making cakes but in Italy, where they are in plentiful supply, walnuts are often used. They give the cupcakes a moist texture as well as a delicious flavor.

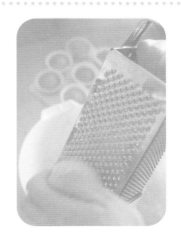

moist walnut cupcakes

Makes 12 cupcakes

³/₄ **cup walnuts**

4 tbsp butter, softened

¹/₂ **cup superfine sugar**

grated rind of ¹/₂ lemon

¹/₂ **cup self-rising white flour**

2 eggs

12 walnut halves, to decorate

Frosting

4 tbsp butter, softened

³/₄ **cup confectioners' sugar**

grated rind of ¹/₂ lemon

I tsp lemon juice

★ Preheat the oven to 375°F/190°C. Put 12 paper baking cases in a muffin pan, or put 12 double-layer paper cases on a baking sheet.

★ Put the walnuts in a food processor and, using a pulsating action, blend until finely ground, being careful not to overgrind, which will turn them to oil. Add the butter, cut into small pieces, along with the sugar, lemon rind, flour, and eggs, then blend until evenly mixed. Spoon the batter into the paper cases.

★ Bake the cupcakes in the preheated oven for 20 minutes, or until well risen and golden brown. Transfer to a wire rack and let cool.

★ To make the frosting, put the butter in a bowl and beat until fluffy. Sift in the confectioners' sugar, add the lemon rind and juice, and mix well together.

★ When the cupcakes are cold, spread the frosting on top of each cupcake and top with a walnut half to decorate.

If you haven't feather-frosted a cake before, you will be surprised how easy it is to do, and the result is very effective.

feather-frosted coffee cupcakes

Makes 16 cupcakes

1 tbsp instant coffee granules

1 tbsp boiling water

8 tbsp butter, softened, or soft margarine

generous ½ cup firmly packed brown sugar

2 eggs

generous ¾ cup self-rising white flour

½ tsp baking powder

2 tbsp sour cream

Frosting

2 cups confectioners' sugar

4 tsp warm water

1 tsp instant coffee granules

2 tsp boiling water

★ Preheat the oven to 375°F/190°C. Put 16 paper baking cases in a muffin pan, or put 16 double-layer paper cases on a baking sheet.

★ Put the coffee granules in a cup or small bowl, add the boiling water, and stir until dissolved. Let cool slightly.

★ Put the butter, sugar, and eggs in a bowl. Sift in the flour and baking powder, then beat the ingredients together until smooth. Add the dissolved coffee and the sour cream and beat together until well mixed. Spoon the batter into the paper cases.

★ Bake the cupcakes in the preheated oven for 20 minutes, or until well risen and golden brown. Transfer to a wire rack and let cool.

★ To make the frosting, sift ¾ cup of the confectioners' sugar into a bowl, then gradually mix in the warm water to make a coating consistency that will cover the back of a wooden spoon. Dissolve the coffee granules in the boiling water. Sift the remaining confectioners' sugar into a bowl, then stir in the dissolved coffee granules. Spoon the frosting into a pastry bag fitted with a piping tip. When the cupcakes are cold, coat the tops with the white frosting, then quickly pipe the coffee frosting in parallel lines on top. Using a skewer, draw it across the piped lines in both directions. Let set before serving.

fruit cupcakes

fruit cupcakes

Coconut and candied cherries make these cakes really moist, and give them a sweet flavor that will make them a hit with children.

coconut cherry cupcakes

Makes 12 cupcakes

8 tbsp butter, softened, or soft
 margarine

generous ¹/₂ cup superfine sugar

2 tbsp milk

2 eggs, lightly beaten

scant ⁵/₈ cup self-rising white flour

¹/₂ tsp baking powder

²/₃ cup dry unsweetened coconut

4 oz/115 g candied cherries,
 quartered

12 whole candied, maraschino, or
 fresh cherries, to decorate

Frosting

4 tbsp butter, softened

1 cup confectioners' sugar

1 tbsp milk

★ Preheat the oven to 350°F/180°C. Put 12 paper baking cases in a muffin pan, or put 12 double-layer paper cases on a baking sheet.

★ Put the butter and sugar in a bowl and beat together until light and fluffy. Stir in the milk. Gradually add the eggs, beating well after each addition. Sift in the flour and baking powder and fold them in with the coconut. Gently fold in most of the quartered cherries. Spoon the batter into the paper cases and sprinkle the remaining quartered cherries on top.

★ Bake the cupcakes in the preheated oven for 20–25 minutes, or until well risen, golden brown, and firm to the touch. Transfer to a wire rack and let cool.

★ To make the buttercream frosting, put the butter in a bowl and beat until fluffy. Sift in the confectioners' sugar and beat together until well mixed, gradually beating in the milk.

★ To decorate the cupcakes, using a pastry bag fitted with a large star tip, pipe the buttercream on top of each cupcake, then add a candied, maraschino, or fresh cherry to decorate.

These are large cupcakes because they are baked in muffin cases—for this delicious recipe, a small cupcake simply wouldn't be enough!

carrot & orange cupcakes with mascarpone frosting

Makes 12 cupcakes

8 tbsp butter, softened, or soft
  margarine

generous ¹/₂ cup firmly packed
  brown sugar

juice and finely grated rind of
  1 small orange

2 large eggs, lightly beaten

6 oz/175 g carrots, grated

¹/₄ cup walnut pieces, coarsely
  chopped

scant 1 cup all-purpose flour

1 tsp ground pumpkin pie spice

1¹/₂ tsp baking powder

Frosting

1¹/₄ cups mascarpone cheese

4 tbsp confectioners' sugar

grated rind of 1 large orange

★ Preheat the oven to 350°F/180°C. Put 12 muffin paper cases in a muffin pan.

★ Put the butter, sugar, and orange rind in a bowl and beat together until light and fluffy. Gradually add the eggs, beating well after each addition. Squeeze any excess liquid from the carrots and add to the mixture with the walnuts and orange juice. Stir into the mixture until well mixed. Sift in the flour, pumpkin pie spice, and baking powder and then, using a metal spoon, fold into the mixture. Spoon the batter into the paper cases.

★ Bake the cupcakes in the preheated oven for 25 minutes, or until well risen, firm to the touch, and golden brown. Transfer to a wire rack and let cool.

★ To make the frosting, put the mascarpone cheese, confectioners' sugar, and orange rind in a large bowl and beat together until well mixed.

★ When the cupcakes are cold, spread the frosting on top of each cupcake, swirling it with a round-bladed knife. Store the cupcakes in the refrigerator until ready to serve.

Butterfly cakes may remind you of children's birthday parties, but these attractive, creamy, miniature delights are popular with adults too.

lemon butterfly cakes

Makes 12 cupcakes

generous ³/₄ cup self-rising white flour

¹/₂ tsp baking powder

8 tbsp soft margarine

generous ¹/₂ cup superfine sugar

2 eggs, lightly beaten

finely grated rind of ¹/₂ lemon

2 tbsp milk

confectioners' sugar, for dusting

Lemon filling

6 tbsp butter, softened

1¹/₂ cups confectioners' sugar

1 tbsp lemon juice

★ Preheat the oven to 375°F/190°C. Put 12 paper baking cases in a muffin pan, or put 12 double-layer paper cases on a baking sheet.

★ Sift the flour and baking powder into a large bowl. Add the margarine, sugar, eggs, lemon rind, and milk and, using an electric hand whisk, beat together until smooth. Spoon the batter into the paper cases.

★ Bake the cupcakes in the preheated oven for 15–20 minutes, or until well risen and golden brown. Transfer to a wire rack and let cool.

★ To make the filling, put the butter in a bowl and beat until fluffy. Sift in the confectioners' sugar, add the lemon juice, and beat together until smooth and creamy.

★ When the cupcakes are cold, use a serrated knife to cut a circle from the top of each cupcake and then cut each circle in half. Spread or pipe a little of the buttercream filling into the center of each cupcake, then press the 2 semicircular halves into it at an angle to resemble butterfly wings. Dust with sifted confectioners' sugar before serving.

These cupcakes are another children's favorite, but the addition of pecans gives them a little sophistication, in case you needed an excuse to try them!

banana & pecan cupcakes

Makes 24 cupcakes

scant 1⁵/8 cups all-purpose flour

1¹/4 tsp baking powder

¹/4 tsp baking soda

2 ripe bananas

8 tbsp butter, softened, or soft margarine

generous ¹/2 cup superfine sugar

¹/2 tsp vanilla extract

2 eggs, lightly beaten

4 tbsp sour cream

¹/2 cup pecans, coarsely chopped

Topping

8 tbsp butter, softened

1 cup confectioners' sugar

¹/4 cup pecans, minced

★ Preheat the oven to 375°F/190°C. Put 24 paper baking cases in a muffin pan, or put 24 double-layer paper cases on a baking sheet.

★ Sift together the flour, baking powder, and baking soda. Peel the bananas, put them in a bowl, and mash with a fork.

★ Put the butter, sugar, and vanilla in a bowl and beat together until light and fluffy. Gradually add the eggs, beating well after each addition. Stir in the mashed bananas and sour cream. Using a metal spoon, fold in the sifted flour mixture and chopped nuts, then spoon the batter into the paper cases.

★ Bake the cupcakes in the preheated oven for 20 minutes, or until well risen and golden brown. Transfer to a wire rack and let cool.

★ To make the topping, put the butter in a bowl and beat until fluffy. Sift in the confectioners' sugar and mix together well. Spread the frosting on top of each cupcake and sprinkle with the minced pecans before serving.

The tartness of the cranberries contrasts really well with the sweetness of these little cakes.

cranberry cupcakes

Makes 14 cupcakes

5¹/₂ tbsp butter, softened, or soft margarine

¹/₂ cup superfine sugar

I large egg

2 tbsp milk

³/₄ cup self-rising flour

I tsp baking powder

scant ³/₄ cup cranberries, frozen

★ Preheat the oven to 350°F/180°C. Put 14 paper baking cases in a muffin pan, or put 14 double-layer paper cases on a baking sheet.

★ Put the butter and sugar in a bowl and beat together until light and fluffy. Gradually beat in the egg, then stir in the milk. Sift in the flour and baking powder and, using a large metal spoon, fold them into the mixture. Gently fold in the frozen cranberries. Spoon the batter into the paper cases.

★ Bake the cupcakes in the preheated oven for 15–20 minutes, or until well risen and golden brown. Transfer to a wire rack and let cool.

These soft, subtly spiced apple cupcakes, topped with a buttery streusel layer, really are very moreish. They are best served warm, if possible.

apple streusel cupcakes

Makes 14 cupcakes

1/2 tsp baking soda

10-oz/280-g jar tart applesauce

4 tbsp butter, softened, or soft margarine

generous 3/8 cup raw brown sugar

1 large egg, lightly beaten

scant 1 1/4 cups self-rising white flour

1/2 tsp ground cinnamon

1/2 tsp freshly ground nutmeg

Topping

generous 1/3 cup all-purpose flour

1/4 cup raw brown sugar

1/4 tsp ground cinnamon

1/4 tsp freshly grated nutmeg

2 1/2 tbsp butter

★ Preheat the oven to 350°F/180°C. Put 14 paper baking cases in a muffin pan, or put 14 double-layer paper cases on a baking sheet.

★ First make the topping. Put the flour, sugar, cinnamon, and nutmeg in a bowl or in the bowl of a food processor. Cut the butter into small pieces, then either rub it in by hand or blend in the processor until the mixture resembles fine bread crumbs. Set aside while you make the cakes.

★ To make the cupcakes, add the baking soda to the jar of applesauce and stir until dissolved. Put the butter and sugar in a bowl and beat together until light and fluffy. Gradually beat in the egg. Sift in the flour, cinnamon, and nutmeg and, using a large metal spoon, fold into the mixture, alternating with the applesauce.

★ Spoon the batter into the paper cases. Sprinkle the topping over each cupcake to cover the tops and press down gently.

★ Bake the cupcakes in the preheated oven for 20 minutes, or until well risen and golden brown. Leave the cakes for 2–3 minutes before serving warm or transfer to a wire rack and let cool.

This recipe shows the true meaning of cupcakes because, as the title suggests, they are baked in a teacup. This also makes them ideal to serve as individual desserts.

warm strawberry cupcakes baked in a teacup

Makes 6 cupcakes

8 tbsp butter, softened, plus extra for greasing

4 tbsp strawberry conserve

generous ¹/₂ cup superfine sugar

2 eggs, lightly beaten

1 tsp vanilla extract

generous ³/₄ cup self-rising white flour

1 lb/450 g small whole fresh strawberries

confectioners' sugar, for dusting

★ Preheat the oven to 350°F/180°C. Grease six heavy, round teacups with butter. Spoon 2 teaspoons of the strawberry conserve in the bottom of each teacup.

★ Put the butter and sugar in a bowl and beat together until light and fluffy. Gradually add the eggs, beating well after each addition, then add the vanilla extract. Sift in the flour and, using a large metal spoon, fold it into the mixture. Spoon the batter into the teacups.

★ Stand the cups in a roasting pan, then pour in enough hot water to come one-third up the sides of the cups. Bake the cupcakes in the preheated oven for 40 minutes, or until well risen and golden brown, and a skewer, inserted in the center, comes out clean. If over-browning, cover the cupcakes with a sheet of foil. Leave the cupcakes to cool for 2–3 minutes, then carefully lift the cups from the pan and place them on saucers.

★ Place a few of the whole strawberries on each cake, then dust them with sifted confectioners' sugar. Serve warm with the remaining strawberries.

Pineapple, flavored with lemon or lime, imbues these cupcakes with a taste of the tropics. For maximum effect, serve them in the afternoon when the sun is shining.

tropical pineapple cupcakes with citrus cream frosting

Makes 12 cupcakes

2 slices of canned pineapple in natural juice

6 tbsp butter, softened, or soft margarine

generous 3/8 cup superfine sugar

1 large egg, lightly beaten

scant 5/8 cup self-rising white flour

1 tbsp juice from the canned pineapple

Frosting

2 tbsp butter, softened

generous 3/8 cup soft cream cheese

grated rind of 1 lemon or lime

scant 1 cup confectioners' sugar

1 tsp lemon juice or lime juice

★ Preheat the oven to 350°F/180°C. Put 12 paper baking cases in a muffin pan, or put 12 double-layer paper cases on a baking sheet.

★ Finely chop the pineapple slices. Put the butter and sugar in a bowl and beat together until light and fluffy. Gradually beat in the egg. Add the flour and, using a large metal spoon, fold into the mixture. Fold in the chopped pineapple and the pineapple juice. Spoon the batter into the paper cases.

★ Bake the cupcakes in the preheated oven for 20 minutes, or until well risen and golden brown. Transfer to a wire rack and let cool.

★ To make the frosting, put the butter and cream cheese in a large bowl and, using an electric hand whisk, beat together until smooth. Add the rind from the lemon or lime. Sift the confectioners' sugar into the mixture, then beat together until well mixed. Gradually beat in the juice from the lemon or lime, adding enough to form a spreading consistency.

★ When the cupcakes are cold, spread the frosting on top of each cake, or fill a pastry bag fitted with a large star tip and pipe the frosting on top. Store the cupcakes in the refrigerator until ready to serve.

Moist with the addition of almonds and flavored with orange, these cupcakes have a final topping of shredded orange rind in syrup, which increases their moistness and enhances their prettiness.

shredded orange cupcakes

Makes 12 cupcakes

6 tbsp butter, softened, or soft margarine

generous 3/8 cup superfine sugar

1 large egg, lightly beaten

scant 5/8 cup self-rising white flour

generous 1/4 cup ground almonds

grated rind and juice of 1 small orange

Orange topping

1 orange

generous 1/4 cup superfine sugar

1/8 cup toasted slivered almonds

★ Preheat the oven to 350°F/180°C. Put 12 paper baking cases in a muffin pan, or put 12 double-layer paper cases on a baking sheet.

★ Put the butter and sugar in a bowl and beat together until light and fluffy. Gradually beat in the egg. Add the flour, ground almonds, and orange rind and, using a large metal spoon, fold into the mixture. Fold in the orange juice. Spoon the batter into the paper cases.

★ Bake the cupcakes in the preheated oven for 20–25 minutes, or until well risen and golden brown.

★ Meanwhile, make the topping. Using a citrus zester, pare the rind from the orange, then squeeze the juice. Put the rind, juice, and sugar in a pan and heat gently, stirring, until the sugar has dissolved, then let simmer for 5 minutes.

★ When the cupcakes have cooked, prick them all over with a skewer. Spoon the warm syrup and rind over each cupcake, then sprinkle the slivered almonds on top. Transfer to a wire rack and let cool.

chocolate sensations

chocolate sensations

Filled with chocolate buttercream, these appealing little cakes are an all-time favorite with both adults and children.

chocolate butterfly cakes

Makes 12 cupcakes

8 tbsp soft margarine

¹/₂ cup superfine sugar

scant 1⁵/₈ cups self-rising white flour

2 large eggs

2 tbsp unsweetened cocoa

1 oz/25 g semisweet chocolate, melted

confectioners' sugar, for dusting

Filling

6 tbsp butter, softened

1¹/₂ cups confectioners' sugar

1 oz/25 g semisweet chocolate, melted

★ Preheat the oven to 350°F/180°C. Put 12 paper baking cases in a muffin pan, or put 12 double-layer paper cases on a baking sheet.

★ Put the margarine, sugar, flour, eggs, and cocoa in a large bowl and, using an electric hand whisk, beat together until just smooth. Beat in the melted chocolate. Spoon the batter into the paper cases, filling them three-fourths full.

★ Bake the cupcakes in the preheated oven for 15 minutes, or until springy to the touch. Transfer to a wire rack and let cool.

★ To make the filling, put the butter in a bowl and beat until fluffy. Sift in the confectioners' sugar and beat together until smooth. Add the melted chocolate and beat together until well mixed.

★ When the cupcakes are cold, use a serrated knife to cut a circle from the top of each cake and then cut each circle in half. Spread or pipe a little of the buttercream into the center of each cupcake and press the 2 semicircular halves into it at an angle to resemble butterfly wings. Dust with sifted confectioners' sugar before serving.

A variation on an old favorite, these delicious little cakes will appeal to both children and grown-ups. Let the cupcakes chill before serving.

chocolate cupcakes with cream cheese frosting

Makes 18 cupcakes

6 tbsp butter, softened, or soft margarine

¹/₂ cup superfine sugar

2 eggs, lightly beaten

2 tbsp milk

¹/₃ cup semisweet chocolate chips

scant 1⁵/₈ cups self-rising white flour

generous ¹/₄ cup unsweetened cocoa

Frosting

8 oz/225 g white chocolate

generous ²/₃ cup lowfat cream cheese

★ Preheat the oven to 400°F/200°C. Put 18 paper baking cases in 2 muffin pans, or put 18 double-layer paper cases on a baking sheet.

★ Put the butter and sugar in a bowl and beat together until light and fluffy. Gradually add the eggs, beating well after each addition. Add the milk, then fold in the chocolate chips. Sift in the flour and cocoa, then fold into the mixture. Spoon the batter into the paper cases and smooth the tops.

★ Bake the cupcakes in the preheated oven for 20 minutes, or until well risen and springy to the touch. Transfer to a wire rack and let cool.

★ To make the frosting, break the chocolate into a small heatproof bowl and set the bowl over a pan of gently simmering water until melted. Let cool slightly. Put the cream cheese in a bowl and beat until softened, then beat in the slightly cooled chocolate.

★ Spread a little of the frosting over the top of each cupcake, then let chill in the refrigerator for 1 hour before serving.

These little, light, and moist cupcakes, with a tempting fudgy chocolate topping, are perfect for serving at any time of day.

dark & white fudge cupcakes

Makes 20 cupcakes

scant 1 cup water

6 tbsp butter

generous 3/8 cup superfine sugar

1 tbsp corn syrup

3 tbsp milk

1 tsp vanilla extract

1 tsp baking soda

scant 1 5/8 cups all-purpose flour

2 tbsp unsweetened cocoa

Topping

1 3/4 oz/50 g semisweet chocolate

4 tbsp water

3 1/2 tbsp butter

1 3/4 oz/50 g white chocolate

3 cups confectioners' sugar

Chocolate curls

3 1/2 oz/100 g semisweet chocolate

3 1/2 oz/100 g white chocolate

★ Preheat the oven to 350°F/180°C. Put 20 paper baking cases in 2 muffin pans, or put 20 double-layer paper cases on 2 baking sheets.

★ Put the water, butter, superfine sugar, and syrup in a pan. Heat gently, stirring, until the sugar has dissolved, then bring to a boil. Reduce the heat and cook gently for 5 minutes. Remove from the heat and let cool.

★ Meanwhile, put the milk and vanilla extract in a bowl. Add the baking soda and stir to dissolve. Sift the flour and cocoa into a separate bowl and add the syrup mixture. Stir in the milk and beat until smooth. Spoon the batter into the paper cases until they are two-thirds full.

★ Bake the cupcakes in the preheated oven for 20 minutes, or until well risen and firm to the touch. Transfer to a wire rack and let cool.

★ To make the topping, break the semisweet chocolate into a small heatproof bowl, add half the water and half the butter, and set the bowl over a pan of gently simmering water until melted. Stir until smooth and let stand over the water. Using another bowl, repeat with the white chocolate and remaining water and butter. Sift half the sugar into each bowl and beat until smooth and thick. Top the cupcakes up with the frostings. Let set. Serve decorated with chocolate curls made by shaving the chocolate with a potato peeler.

These cupcakes, bursting with chocolate chips, are always irresistible to children so, by baking them in muffin cases, these large versions should be especially satisfying.

jumbo chocolate chip cupcakes

Makes 8 cupcakes

7 tbsp soft margarine

1/2 cup superfine sugar

2 large eggs

scant 3/4 cup self-rising white flour

generous 1/2 cup semisweet chocolate chips

★ Preheat the oven to 375°F/190°C. Put 8 muffin paper cases in a muffin pan.

★ Put the margarine, sugar, eggs, and flour in a large bowl and, using an electric hand whisk, beat together until just smooth. Fold in the chocolate chips. Spoon the batter into the paper cases.

★ Bake the cupcakes in the preheated oven for 20–25 minutes, or until well risen and golden brown. Transfer to a wire rack to cool.

There is always something fascinating about the look of marbled cakes and it is from their appearance that they get their name. When they are cut or bitten into, each slice or bite shows the swirling of feathered Italian marble.

marbled chocolate cupcakes

Makes 21 cupcakes

³/₄ **cup soft margarine**

generous ³/₄ **cup superfine sugar**

3 **eggs**

scant 1¹/₄ **cups self-rising white flour**

2 **tbsp milk**

2 oz/55 g **semisweet chocolate, melted**

★ Preheat the oven to 350°F/180°C. Put 21 paper baking cases in a muffin pan, or put 21 double-layer paper cases on a baking sheet.

★ Put the margarine, sugar, eggs, flour, and milk in a large bowl and, using an electric hand whisk, beat together until just smooth.

★ Divide the batter between 2 bowls. Add the melted chocolate to one bowl and stir together until well mixed. Using a teaspoon, and alternating the chocolate batter with the plain batter, put four half-teaspoons into each paper case.

★ Bake the cupcakes in the preheated oven for 20 minutes, or until well risen and springy to the touch. Transfer to a wire rack and let cool.

Chocolate chunks packed inside a cupcake produce an irresistible molten-chocolate center, and they are served warm so that the chocolate really does melt in your mouth.

warm molten-centered chocolate cupcakes

Makes 8 cupcakes

4 tbsp soft margarine

generous ¼ cup superfine sugar

1 large egg

scant ⅝ cup self-rising flour

1 tbsp unsweetened cocoa

2 oz/55 g semisweet chocolate

confectioners' sugar, for dusting

★ Preheat the oven to 375°F/190°C. Put 8 paper baking cases in a muffin pan, or put 8 double-layer paper cases on a baking sheet.

★ Put the margarine, sugar, egg, flour, and cocoa in a large bowl and, using an electric hand whisk, beat together until just smooth.

★ Spoon half of the batter into the paper cases. Using a teaspoon, make an indentation in the center of each cake. Break the chocolate evenly into 8 squares and place a piece in each indentation, then spoon the remaining cake batter on top.

★ Bake the cupcakes in the preheated oven for 20 minutes, or until well risen and springy to the touch. Leave the cupcakes for 2–3 minutes before serving warm, dusted with sifted confectioners' sugar.

These pretty little cupcakes are perfect for serving with coffee after dinner. Alternatively, packed into an attractive box, they make a lovely homemade gift. You will find mini paper cases in specialized cake decoration stores.

tiny chocolate cupcakes with ganache frosting

Makes 20 cupcakes

4 tbsp butter, softened

generous ¼ cup superfine sugar

I large egg, lightly beaten

scant ½ cup white self-rising flour

2 tbsp unsweetened cocoa

I tbsp milk

20 chocolate-coated coffee beans, to decorate (optional)

Frosting

3½ oz/100 g semisweet chocolate

generous ⅓ cup heavy cream

★ Preheat the oven to 375°F/190°C. Put 20 double-layer mini paper cases on 2 baking sheets.

★ Put the butter and sugar in a bowl and beat together until light and fluffy. Gradually beat in the egg. Sift in the flour and cocoa and then, using a metal spoon, fold them into the mixture. Stir in the milk.

★ Fill a pastry bag, fitted with a large plain tip, with the batter and pipe it into the paper cases, filling each one until half full.

★ Bake the cakes in the preheated oven for 10–15 minutes, or until well risen and firm to the touch. Transfer to a wire rack to cool.

★ To make the frosting, break the chocolate into a pan and add the cream. Heat gently, stirring all the time, until the chocolate has melted. Pour into a large heatproof bowl and, using an electric hand whisk, beat the mixture for 10 minutes, or until thick, glossy and cool.

★ Fill a pastry bag, fitted with a large star tip, with the frosting and pipe a swirl on top of each cupcake. Alternatively, spoon the frosting over the top of each cupcake. Chill in the refrigerator for I hour before serving. Serve decorated with a chocolate-coated coffee bean, if liked.

The first recorded recipe for Devil's Food Chocolate Cake is from 1905 and its name is thought to have come from the fact that it is so rich and indulgent that it must be wicked and evil. Miniature versions of this classic American cake make them even more irresistible.

devil's food cakes with chocolate frosting

Makes 18 cupcakes

3¹/2 tbsp soft margarine

generous 1/2 cup firmly packed brown sugar

2 large eggs

generous 3/4 cup all-purpose flour

1/2 tsp baking soda

generous 1/4 cup unsweetened cocoa

1/2 cup sour cream

Frosting

4¹/2 oz/125 g semisweet chocolate

2 tbsp superfine sugar

2/3 cup sour cream

Chocolate curls (optional)

3¹/2 oz/100 g semisweet chocolate

★ Preheat the oven to 350°F/180°C. Put 18 paper baking cases in a muffin pan, or put 18 double-layer paper cases on a baking sheet.

★ Put the margarine, sugar, eggs, flour, baking soda, and cocoa in a large bowl and, using an electric hand whisk, beat together until just smooth. Using a metal spoon, fold in the sour cream. Spoon the batter into the paper cases.

★ Bake the cupcakes in the preheated oven for 20 minutes, or until well risen and firm to the touch. Transfer to a wire rack to cool.

★ To make the frosting, break the chocolate into a heatproof bowl. Set the bowl over a pan of gently simmering water and heat until melted, stirring occasionally. Remove from the heat and let cool slightly, then whisk in the sugar and sour cream until combined. Spread the frosting over the tops of the cupcakes and let set in the refrigerator before serving. If liked, serve decorated with chocolate curls made by shaving semisweet chocolate with a potato peeler.

These cupcakes look like little cups of cappuccino coffee and are perfect for serving with midmorning coffee.

mocha cupcakes with whipped cream

Makes 20 cupcakes

2 tbsp instant espresso coffee powder

6 tbsp butter

generous 3/8 cup superfine sugar

I tbsp honey

scant I cup water

scant I5/8 cups all-purpose flour

2 tbsp unsweetened cocoa

I tsp baking soda

3 tbsp milk

I large egg, lightly beaten

Topping

I cup whipping cream

unsweetened cocoa, sifted, for dusting

★ Preheat the oven to 350°F/180°C. Put 20 paper baking cases in 2 muffin pans, or put 20 double-layer paper cases on 2 baking sheets.

★ Put the coffee powder, butter, sugar, honey, and water in a pan and heat gently, stirring, until the sugar has dissolved. Bring to a boil, then reduce the heat and let simmer for 5 minutes. Pour into a large heatproof bowl and let cool.

★ When the mixture has cooled, sift in the flour and cocoa. Dissolve the baking soda in the milk, then add to the mixture with the egg and beat together until smooth. Spoon the batter into the paper cases.

★ Bake the cupcakes in the preheated oven for 15–20 minutes, or until well risen and firm to the touch. Transfer to a wire rack to cool.

★ For the topping, whisk the cream in a bowl until it holds its shape. Just before serving, spoon heaping teaspoonfuls of cream on top of each cake, then dust lightly with sifted cocoa. Store the cupcakes in the refrigerator until ready to serve.

festive creations

festive creations

Children will love to get their fangs into these little cakes.
They will enjoy decorating them with creepy spiders too.

halloween cupcakes

Makes 12 cupcakes

8 tbsp soft margarine

generous ½ cup superfine sugar

2 eggs

generous ¾ cup self-rising white flour

Topping

7 oz/200 g orange ready-to-roll colored fondant frosting

confectioners' sugar, for dusting

2 oz/55 g black ready-to-roll colored fondant frosting

black cake writing frosting

white cake writing frosting

★ Preheat the oven to 350°F/180°C. Put 12 paper baking cases in a muffin pan, or put 12 double-layer paper cases on a baking sheet.

★ Put the margarine, sugar, eggs, and flour in a bowl and, using an electric hand whisk, beat together until smooth. Spoon the batter into the cases.

★ Bake the cupcakes in the preheated oven for 15–20 minutes, or until well risen, golden brown, and firm to the touch. Transfer to a wire rack and let cool.

★ When the cupcakes are cold, knead the orange frosting until pliable, then roll out on a counter dusted with confectioners' sugar. Using the palm of your hand, lightly rub confectioners' sugar into the frosting to prevent it from spotting. Using a 2¼-inch/5.5-cm plain round cutter, cut out 12 circles, rerolling the frosting as necessary. Place a circle on top of each cupcake.

★ Roll out the black frosting on a counter lightly dusted with confectioners' sugar. Using the palm of your hand, lightly rub confectioners' sugar into the frosting to prevent it from spotting. Using a 1¼-inch/3-cm plain round cutter, cut out 12 circles and place them on the center of the cupcakes. Using black writing frosting, pipe 8 legs on to each spider and using white writing frosting, draw 2 eyes and a mouth.

The 14th of February was probably chosen as Valentine's Day because it was the ancient belief that birds, particularly lovebirds, began to mate on that date. Make a batch of these delicious cupcakes for the one you love. Alternatively, impress your family and friends with them.

valentine heart cupcakes

Makes 6 cupcakes

6 tbsp butter, softened, or soft margarine

generous 3/8 cup superfine sugar

1/2 tsp vanilla extract

2 eggs, lightly beaten

1/2 cup all-purpose flour

I tbsp unsweetened cocoa

I tsp baking powder

Marzipan hearts

1 1/4 oz/35 g marzipan

red food coloring (liquid or paste)

confectioners' sugar, for dusting

Topping

4 tbsp butter, softened

I cup confectioners' sugar

I oz/25 g semisweet chocolate, melted

6 chocolate flower decorations

★ To make the hearts, knead the marzipan until pliable, then add a few drops of red coloring and knead until evenly colored red. Roll out the marzipan to a thickness of 1/4 inch/5 mm on a counter dusted with confectioners' sugar. Using a small heart-shaped cutter, cut out 6 hearts. Put these on a tray lined with waxed paper and dusted with confectioners' sugar. Let dry for 3–4 hours.

★ To make the cupcakes, preheat the oven to 350°F/180°C. Put 6 paper muffin cases in a muffin pan.

★ Put the butter, sugar, and vanilla extract in a bowl and beat together until light and fluffy. Gradually add the eggs, beating well after each addition. Sift in the flour, cocoa, and baking powder and, using a large metal spoon, fold into the mixture. Spoon the batter into the paper cases.

★ Bake the cupcakes in the preheated oven for 20–25 minutes, or until well risen and firm to the touch. Transfer to a wire rack and let cool.

★ To make the topping, put the butter in a large bowl and beat until fluffy. Sift in the confectioners' sugar and beat together until smooth. Add the melted chocolate and beat together until well mixed. When the cakes are cold, spread the frosting on top of each cake and decorate with a chocolate flower.

These cupcakes are baked in muffin cases so that they are larger than the usual cupcakes. Once decorated, they look like miniature Christmas cakes. The addition of ground almonds gives a firm texture and adds a richness suitable for the occasion.

christmas cupcakes

Makes 16 cupcakes

9 tbsp butter, softened

I cup superfine sugar

4–6 drops almond extract

4 eggs, lightly beaten

generous I cup self-rising white flour

1 3/4 cups ground almonds

Topping

I lb/450 g white ready-to-roll fondant frosting

2 oz/55 g green ready-to-roll colored fondant frosting

I oz/25 g red ready-to-roll colored fondant frosting

confectioners' sugar, for dusting

★ Preheat the oven to 350°F/180°C. Put 16 paper muffin cases in a muffin pan.

★ Put the butter, sugar, and almond extract in a bowl and beat together until light and fluffy. Gradually add the eggs, beating well after each addition. Add the flour and, using a large metal spoon, fold it into the mixture, then fold in the ground almonds. Spoon the batter into the paper cases to half-fill them.

★ Bake the cakes in the preheated oven for 20 minutes, or until well risen, golden brown, and firm to the touch. Transfer to a wire rack and let cool.

★ When the cakes are cold, knead the white frosting until pliable, then roll out on a counter lightly dusted with confectioners' sugar. Using a 2¾-inch/7-cm plain round cutter, cut out 16 circles, rerolling the frosting as necessary. Place a circle on top of each cupcake.

★ Roll out the green frosting on a counter lightly dusted with confectioners' sugar. Using the palm of your hand, rub confectioners' sugar into the frosting to prevent it from spotting. Using a holly leaf-shaped cutter, cut out 32 leaves, rerolling the frosting as necessary. Brush each leaf with a little cooled boiled water and place 2 leaves on top of each cake. Roll the red frosting between the palms of your hands to form 48 berries and place in the center of the leaves.

These cupcakes are made with a basic plain base and a pretty frosted top. They are perfect for children's parties—so wonderfully light and delicate that you can have more than one—but they are also so easy to make that you can make more than enough for everyone.

birthday party cupcakes

Makes 24 cupcakes

1 cup soft margarine

generous 1¹/₈ cups superfine sugar

4 eggs

scant 1⁵/₈ cups self-rising white flour

Topping

³/₄ cup butter, softened

3 cups confectioners' sugar

a variety of small sweets and chocolates, sugar-coated chocolates, dried fruits, edible sugar flower shapes, cake decorating sprinkles, silver dragées (cake decoration balls), and sugar strands

various colored tubes of writing frosting

24 birthday cake candles (optional)

silver dragées (cake decoration balls)

★ Preheat the oven to 350°F/180°C. Put 24 paper baking cases in a muffin pan, or put 24 double-layer paper cases on a baking sheet.

★ Put the margarine, sugar, eggs, and flour in a large bowl and, using an electric hand whisk, beat together until just smooth. Spoon the batter into the paper cases.

★ Bake the cupcakes in the preheated oven for 15–20 minutes, or until well risen, golden brown, and firm to the touch. Transfer to a wire rack and let cool.

★ To make the frosting, put the butter in a bowl and beat until fluffy. Sift in the confectioners' sugar and beat together until smooth and creamy.

★ When the cupcakes are cold, spread the frosting on top of each cupcake, then decorate to your choice and, if desired, place a candle in the top of each.

Easter eggs have been part of Easter festivities for a long time. Miniature chocolate eggs, nestled on top of chocolate cupcakes, are the perfect treat for the Easter vacation.

easter cupcakes

Makes 12 cupcakes

8 tbsp butter, softened, or soft margarine

generous ¹/₂ cup superfine sugar

2 eggs, lightly beaten

scant ⁵/₈ cup self-rising white flour

generous ¹/₄ cup unsweetened cocoa

Topping

6 tbsp butter, softened

1¹/₂ cups confectioners' sugar

1 tbsp milk

2–3 drops of vanilla extract

two 4³/₄-oz/130-g packages mini chocolate candy shell eggs

★ Preheat the oven to 350°F/180°C. Put 12 paper baking cases in a muffin pan, or put 12 double-layer paper cases on a baking sheet.

★ Put the butter and sugar in a bowl and beat together until light and fluffy. Gradually add the eggs, beating well after each addition. Sift in the flour and cocoa and, using a large metal spoon, fold into the mixture. Spoon the batter into the paper cases.

★ Bake the cupcakes in the preheated oven for 15–20 minutes, or until well risen and firm to the touch. Transfer to a wire rack and let cool.

★ To make the buttercream topping, put the butter in a bowl and beat until fluffy. Sift in the confectioners' sugar and beat together until well mixed, adding the milk and vanilla extract.

★ When the cupcakes are cold, put the frosting in a pastry bag, fitted with a large star tip, and pipe a circle around the edge of each cupcake to form a nest. Place chocolate eggs in the center of each nest, to decorate.

It doesn't need to be a golden or silver anniversary to serve these beautiful cupcakes. Any anniversary or festive celebration will do. Look for silver or gold foil cake cases in cake decoration stores.

gold & silver anniversary cupcakes

Makes 24 cupcakes

1 cup butter, softened

generous 1 cup superfine sugar

1 tsp vanilla extract

4 large eggs, lightly beaten

scant 1⁵/₈ cups self-rising white flour

5 tbsp milk

Topping

³/₄ cup unsalted butter

3 cups confectioners' sugar

silver or gold dragées (cake decoration balls)

★ Preheat the oven to 350°F/180°C. Put 24 silver or gold foil cake cases in muffin pans, or arrange them on baking sheets.

★ Put the butter, sugar, and vanilla extract in a bowl and beat together until light and fluffy. Gradually add the eggs, beating well after each addition. Add the flour and, using a large metal spoon, fold into the mixture with the milk. Spoon the batter into the paper cases.

★ Bake the cupcakes in the preheated oven for 15–20 minutes, or until well risen and firm to the touch. Transfer to a wire rack and let cool.

★ To make the topping, put the butter in a large bowl and beat until fluffy. Sift in the confectioners' sugar and beat together until well mixed. Put the topping in a pastry bag, fitted with a medium star-shaped tip.

★ When the cupcakes are cold, pipe icing on top of each cupcake to cover the tops. Sprinkle over the silver or gold dragées before serving.

Baby shower parties allow your family and friends to share the joy and excitement of welcoming a new life into the world. To frost these cupcakes, you could choose pink for a girl or blue for a boy.

baby shower cupcakes with sugared almonds

Makes 24 cupcakes

1³/₄ cups butter, softened

2 cups superfine sugar

finely grated rind of 2 lemons

8 eggs, lightly beaten

generous 2³/₄ cups self-rising white flour

Topping

3 cups confectioners' sugar

red or blue food coloring (liquid or paste)

24 sugared almonds

★ Preheat the oven to 350°F/180°C. Put 24 paper muffin cases in a muffin pan.

★ Put the butter, sugar, and lemon rind in a bowl and beat together until light and fluffy. Gradually add the eggs, beating well after each addition. Add the flour and, using a large metal spoon, fold into the mixture. Spoon the batter into the paper cases to half-fill them.

★ Bake the cupcakes in the preheated oven for 20–25 minutes, or until well risen, golden brown, and firm to the touch. Transfer to a wire rack and let cool.

★ When the cakes are cold, make the topping. Sift the confectioners' sugar into a bowl. Add 6–8 teaspoons of hot water and stir until the mixture is smooth and thick enough to coat the back of a wooden spoon. Dip a skewer into the red or blue food coloring, then stir it into the frosting until it is evenly colored pink or pale blue.

★ Spoon the frosting on top of each cupcake. Top each with a sugared almond and let set for about 30 minutes before serving.

This stunning centerpiece is a festive cake with a difference, since each guest has his or her own individual cupcake. If you are inviting more than 48 guests, just increase the number of cupcakes you make.

the cupcake wedding cake

Makes 48 cupcakes

1 lb/450 g butter, softened

1 lb/450 g superfine sugar

2 tsp vanilla extract

8 large eggs, lightly beaten

1 lb/450 g self-rising white flour

²/₃ cup milk

Topping

1 lb 4 oz/550 g confectioners' sugar

48 ready-made sugar roses, or 48 small fresh rosebuds gently rinsed and left to dry on paper towels

To assemble the cake

one 20-inch/50-cm, one 16-inch/40-cm, one 12-inch/ 30-cm, and one 8-inch/ 20-cm sandblasted glass disk with polished edges, or 4 silver cake boards

13 white or Perspex cake pillars

1 small bouquet of fresh flowers in a small vase

★ Preheat the oven to 350°F/180°C. Put 48 paper baking cases in a muffin pan, or put 48 double-layer paper cases on a baking sheet.

★ Put the butter, sugar, and vanilla extract in a bowl and beat together until light and fluffy. Gradually add the eggs, beating well after each addition. Add the flour and, using a large metal spoon, fold into the mixture with the milk. Spoon the batter into the paper cases.

★ Bake the cupcakes in the preheated oven for 15–20 minutes, or until well risen and firm to the touch. Transfer to a wire rack and let cool.

★ To make the topping, sift the confectioners' sugar into a large bowl. Add 3–4 tablespoons hot water and stir until the mixture is smooth and thick enough to coat the back of a wooden spoon. Spoon the frosting on top of each cupcake. Store the cupcakes in an airtight container for up to one day.

★ On the day of serving, carefully place a sugar rose or rosebud on top of each cupcake. To arrange the cupcakes, place the largest disk or board on a table where the finished display is to be. Stand 5 pillars on the disk and arrange some of the cupcakes on the base. Continue with the remaining bases, pillars (using only 4 pillars to support each remaining tier), and cupcakes to make 4 tiers, standing the bouquet of flowers in the center of the top tier.

index